LET'S STAY TOGETHER

TOGETHER

WHY YES TO EUROPE

DENIS MACSHANE

I.B. TAURIS

LONDON · NEW YORK

Published in 2016 by
I.B. Tauris & Co. Ltd
London • New York
www.ibtauris.com

ISBN: 978 1 78453 728 9
eISBN: 978 1 78672 060 3
ePDF: 978 1 78673 060 2

A full CIP record for this book is available from the British Library

A full CIP record is available from the Library of Congress
Library of Congress Catalog Card Number: available

Typeset by Out of House Publishing
Printed and bound by TJ International Ltd, Padstow, PL28 8RW

MIX
Paper from
responsible sources
FSC® C013056

CONTENTS

CONTENTS

INTRODUCTION

The main purpose of this book is both political and emotional. I believe we can have our country and our Europe. I will advance the case that there is no contradiction between being pro-British and pro-European. But if we choose to revert to the great British temptation of isolationism then we will both weaken Britain and undermine our friends, partners and allies across the Channel and the Irish Sea.

I will discuss some of the economic arguments in due course, but this is my sense about the identity of my country and the Britain I want my children, all now in their twenties, to live in. It is a letter to them and their generation to explain how lucky I think I have been to live in a Britain that, for most of my adult life, has cooperated and integrated with other European countries.

In 2007, the *Independent* announced on its front page '50 Reasons to Love the EU'. I wrote these reasons and the then editor, Simon Kelner, who liked shock front pages, published my list.

There were more on the inside pages, under the Monty Python-style heading 'What Has Europe Ever Done for You?' Here are the first four:

1   The end of war between European nations
2   Democracy flourishing (more or less) in 28 countries
3   Once-poor countries have had a long period of prosperity
4   The creation of the world's largest internal trading market

... and you can read all of them at the back of this booklet.

In recent years, arguments in favour of Europe have been thinner and thinner on the ground. Taken as a whole this century, the British Establishment – the main newspapers, the Conservative Party, key opinion formers and many of the controllers of our economy – has found much to complain about and condemn in the functioning of the European Union (EU). The Establishment has rarely paused for a moment to ask if its disappearance would be good for Britain or indeed to balance criticism by permitting arguments that defend Europe. I discuss the different currents of hostility to Europe in my book *Brexit: How Britain Will Leave Europe*, first published by I.B.Tauris in February 2015 and updated following Mr Cameron's re-election as prime minister in May 2015 and the formal decision to organize the referendum on 23 June 2016.

Establishment hostility to Europe from the late 1990s onwards transcended politics. In recent months the *Guardian* newspaper, for example, has carried pieces by its star commentators like Sir Simon Jenkins, Paul Mason, Owen Jones and Giles Fraser attacking the EU, with some calling for Britain to leave.

Many of the left-liberal political and economic commentators rubbished the euro and seemed to believe that a Europe of competing, devaluing, protectionist currencies, including the pound sterling, was better than the single currency.

In recent years big and small business have complained about the European Commission. Regulations to stop employees from being killed or injured at work, or to ban the use of asbestos, or to prevent discrimination against pregnant women or workers with disabilities, were presented as an onerous burden.

The Confederation of British Industry (CBI) in 2013 called for a permanent opt-out from the Working Time Directive even though Britain has an opt-out allowing employees to work more than 48 hours a week. Firms in Germany or the Netherlands were profitable and had better productivity records than their British counterparts, but did not feel the need to always blame the EU for any failings of their management culture.

In 2009, the British Chambers of Commerce (BCC) claimed that EU regulations cost its members £11 billion a year, without pointing out that rules are needed not only to protect British consumers but also to open up the entire EU market. In 2007, the Institute of Directors produced a long critical report of the EU Lisbon Treaty complaining that some policies would be decided by majority voting – which is at the core of the single market, which would never have come into being and will never be completed if national parliaments maintain protectionist rights to veto any Europe-wide policy to promote competition.

Before 2010 there were many in the business world who were unhappy at the constant chip, chip, chip at the EU from business organizations but didn't want to enter into conflict with their friends in the Conservative Party, especially before 2010, when Conservatives daily attacked the two Labour prime ministers for any agreements reached with their fellow heads of EU governments.

Since David Cameron's announcement of his Brexit plebiscite in January 2013, I have from time to time suggested to business leaders that perhaps they should make some statement against Brexit. But the reply was usually that they preferred not to enter political or controversial arguments. The CBI is now officially opposing Brexit but will not sign up to the campaign. The Director-General of BCC resigned after being suspended when he came out as a devout Brexit supporter. The BCC now says it will be neutral on the issue.

I have written many articles tackling the errors and the at times untruthful propaganda of the anti-EU Establishment. But they remain unpublished in my MacBook files as newspapers and political weeklies like the *New Statesman* had editors who refused to make the case for the EU. I did not worry for myself as there are many with better writing or advocacy skills, but so strong was the anti-EU Establishment in Britain that those supporting the EU were denied a platform to make their case in the face of the daily outpouring of anti-EU arguments and comments in recent years.

In the 1930s, Lord Northcliffe, owner of *The Times*, and his editor, Geoffrey Dawson, supported British isolationists who believed

Britain should stay aloof from continental engagement. They made sure nothing was allowed into *The Times* and other papers like the *Daily Mail* or *Daily Express* which challenged the isolationist Establishment view on Europe at the time. So too in our time we have owners and senior editors of our press that are part of the anti-EU Establishment and actively promote the isolation of our country from present-day Europe as organized in the EU.

I hope that by now members or supporters of the BNP, UKIP and Europhobe Tories and *Daily Mail* journalists will have stopped reading. I promise they will disagree with every word to come. And since I am a happy, easy-going chap who has always got on well with Nigel Farage and his Scouse deputy, Paul Nuttall MEP, and remember warmly that the anti-EU Tory Daniel Hannam was one of the few men willing to state publicly his dismay at my ousting from politics, I do not want to upset the men and women who have a different view on Europe but with whom I have enjoyed debating.

So, please – Boris (Johnson), Michael (Gove), Nigel (Farage) and Bill (Cash) and Douglas (Carswell) and Simon (Heffer) and Tim (Montgomerie) – don't read this. Stay true to your beliefs as I'll stay true to mine, and whether 'In' or 'Out' we can still meet, have a drink and talk about what happens next.

I love my country – but there are plenty of writers and politicians to express that affection. I also love Europe and the idea of union in Europe. This is my expression of that affection, even *amour*.

PART ONE

1

CIVIS EUROPEUS SUM

The 50 points in favour of the EU that I jotted down and that the *Independent* published in 2007 is not a narrow list of reasons to vote 'Yes' or 'Remain' in the referendum, nor really much based on the traditional economic and trade arguments. Read it as one man's love affair with this maddening, beautiful, devious, deadly and delightful part of the world where we live willy-nilly and are condemned to live whether or not we stay in the EU.

It is about growing up with a Polish father who took a bullet in his shoulder fighting in 1939, and an Irish-Scottish mother: my childhood was spent in a historical world of Polish, Irish and Scottish nations forever subjugated by the English, the Germans or the Russians.

Yet my culture is entirely English. A Benedictine school in Ealing, Oxford, the BBC: everything that makes me comes from England. This is reinforced by years as a South Yorkshire MP, as there is no part of England more English than Rotherham, Sheffield, Doncaster and Barnsley.

Yet for all that I am European. Just as the proud Roman said *civis Romanus sum* while still coming from what today we call Spain, France or Greece, I am proud to declare *civis Europeus sum*. I am a European citizen and a British citizen, Scots by birth, English by upbringing, Polish and Irish in blood and thus a member of what Defoe called the mongrel race – the only race in the world worth belonging to.

My four children are even more mongrel, with a Vietnamese grandpapa, a French grandmother, holders of British and French passports, eligible by birth to become Swiss and yet united with all their distant relatives from Donegal to Lublin by being European.

Their grandparents and ancestors before that grew up in a very different Europe of bickering, quarrelling, often warring states and nations that for a millennium and a half after the end of the great Roman Europe could never live at peace one with another.

We killed each other because we were French not Germans, Scots not English, Irish not British, Serbs not Kosovans, Catholics not Protestants, white not brown, Jews not Christians, left-wingers not liberals, Republicans not Royalists, men not women, communists not fascists, southerners not northerners.

In *Gulliver's Travels*, Jonathan Swift mocked the war between those who insisted a boiled egg should be opened at its pointed end and those who rejected such an evil proposition and said the law should permit an egg to be cracked open only at its round end.

This was early eighteenth-century satire, but after the 50-year peace imposed in 1648 by the Treaty of Westphalia which ended the Catholic–Protestant, Franco-Germanic Thirty Years War, the wars of Europe were only just getting under way, culminating in the long civil war of 1914–1945. (Brendan Simms, Cambridge University Professor of the History of International Relations, has written a fine survey of the way pre-EU nations fought themselves to death: *Europe: The Struggle for Supremacy 1453 to the Present*, Penguin, 2014.)

To be sure, there were high achievements in art, writing, architecture, science, music, but every few decades Europe got back to what its disunited nations and people seemed unable to avoid. It was about the violence of war. In the *Marseillaise*, throats are slit and blood flows into the furrow of fields. This may be a stirring tune when sung in the movie *Casablanca* or at Wembley Stadium after the Paris atrocities, but its words celebrate the shedding of blood that would please any mass murderer.

Even the English Christian hymn 'Onward Christian soldiers, marching as to war' fits into the European heritage of doing good by killing as many as possible. It is no accident that the hymn was written at the high moment of British imperialism, which was as much based on war and conquest as any empire in history. The Wehrmacht soldier in World War II had on his army-issue belt buckle the words *Gott mit Uns* – God with Us – as he guarded German extermination camps in Poland.

Can we not create a twenty-first-century Europe where those invocations of national supremacy belong to the history books?

2
IT'S EMOTION, STUPID

Now that Prime Minister David Cameron has rightly decided that for Britain to isolate itself from Europe would be foolish and is therefore calling for a 'Remain' vote in the referendum, the media moguls, their editors and top writers are beside themselves with anger in their attacks on him. The siren calls for isolation and turning our backs on Europe are as strong today from the Establishment as they were in the 1930s.

If the Brexit isolationists and the anti-EU Establishment are defeated in the referendum it will be a great victory for common sense and democracy in Britain. It will show those with power and limitless money that to try and buy public opinion and dictate the decisions our nation takes can be challenged and defeated.

Those campaigning to prevent a victory for the isolationists supporting Brexit are advancing many arguments based on solid data about the economic damage to Britain of losing EU membership with its unfettered, unqualified access to the single market of 500 million, mainly middle-class, consumers. A few firms with investments in our country are now writing to their employees expressing fears about what Brexit might entail. Economists specializing in currency movements foresee a sharp reduction in the value of the pound sterling – possibly to parity between the pound and the euro – £1 = €1. It would be a grim irony indeed if the Brexit campaigners managed to make the pound the same as the euro!

I respect the point of view of anti-Europeans, and if truth be told often enjoy the sharpness of their arguments more than the rather turgid enthusiasms of obsessive Europhiles. As a combative polemicist all my life, a rule-breaker rather than a rule-taker, I would love to embrace Euroscepticism, whose advocates are often sharper of pen and mouth than those of us who reject isolationism.

But as powerful as the anti-EU Establishment is and alluring as is the money paid to its chief promoters, I prefer to stay with my truth that to see Britain turn its back on European union (and the EU) would not be right for my country.

My Europe is one in which the nations of this continent have never had it so good until recently.

A ten-point summary of why I think we should stay in the EU would go something like this:

1   Britain has always made its living by trade. Half our exports go to the EU and to stop being a rule-maker about EU trade and instead be turned into a rule-taker makes no sense.

2   Working to complement each other, NATO and the EU have ensured a Europe free of armed conflict. The European nations of my youth under fascist control and the nations that remained under Soviet domination are now all free, democratic and strong thanks to EU membership. It is one thing for a small nation like Norway or Switzerland to opt not to join the EU, but a country the size of Britain walking out would reinforce nationalist, populist forces elsewhere in Europe that want a Europe established on national, ethnic and sometimes religious bases – the old Europe of hates and conflicts.

3   If Germany has the automobile business, France the luxury goods and agro-exporting business and Spain, Italy and Greece the mass tourism business, our EU specialism is financial services. To risk losing that would be bad for national income. And without the right of the single EU passport for financial trade London would suffer as new rules transferred euro-denominated trades to within the eurozone.

4   The challenges of people movement cannot be met by one nation alone. The United States has 11 million illegal immigrants despite border fences and all sorts of anti-immigrant measures. The EU must strengthen its external borders and export capital and job-creating investment instead of the military intervention-ism of recent years that turned nations like Iraq, Libya and Syria into refugee-producing and people-trafficking centres. Britain cannot alone find solutions to mass people movements.

5   Two million of our citizens live, work or have retired in other EU member states. Anyone tried to get a visa for Australia or a work permit for America? As members of the EU we can live and work anywhere in Europe without let or hindrance, with all the rights of local national citizens. Brexit would at best reduce, at worst remove those rights, so that British citizens might be forced to return home.

6   The total EU income is just 1 per cent of Europe's gross national income. About 85 per cent of it goes back to national governments in the form of farmer subsidies and help for poorer regions in the UK like Cornwall or, in the 1990s, South Yorkshire. Today South Wales with its de-industrialized mass youth unemployment has received £800 million from the EU to support social and economic development. The income that is under the control of the differ-ent EU institutions is about one sixth of 1 per cent of Europe's GDP. For that modest outlay we get a lot of benefits, including £650 million a year of EU funds for scientific and other research in British universities. I want to keep that money flowing in.

7   Brexit would either end or put in jeopardy the student exchanges, Erasmus scholarships, rights of low-cost airlines to land anywhere under single-market regulations and cheaper mobile phone calls that the EU has made other countries accept. After Brexit there would be no more EU Health Card. Currently if I need urgent health care treatment in any EU nation I get it without taking out costly insurance or forking out a fortune as in the USA.

8   Brexit would end the automatic obligation on EU member states to return to Britain any criminal wanted by our police.

After the 7/7 London bombings by Islamists, one of the terrorists escaped to Rome. Due to the European Arrest Warrant system he was sent back to London. By contrast, an Algerian Islamist terrorist wanted by France for his part in the 1995 Paris Metro bombing was protected in London by lawyers and judges for ten years as the European Arrest Warrant was not in existence in 1995. After Brexit, criminals escaping Britain would breathe easier. Crime is now transfrontier, and an exit from police and judicial cooperation mandated by EU rules would not be good for British citizens.

9   Air pollution, climate change and filthy beaches respect no national rules. Thanks to the EU we have had to clean up our beaches and raise standards on combating global warming. Of course it can always be argued that such improvements can happen at national level and be imposed by national law. But suppose a neighbouring nation doesn't want to cooperate or indeed the many vested interests in our own country refuse to raise standards? Brexit would worsen the chances of enforced and enforceable policy and rules on handing on a better environment to future generations.

10 We are going through a revolution in the world of work. Robots and new technology are killing jobs, and it is harder than ever to find the right policies that promote investment and secure good returns for capital and adequate pay for citizens so that they can lead fair and decent lives. Inequality between and within most nations, especially intergenerational inequality, is rising, bringing new tensions and quarrels between haves and have-nots. Brexit, with the abolition of Social Europe obligations that make the EU the only world region which mandates fair treatment of citizens at work, would increase the tendency to a less fair, more unequal Britain. We either love one another or die, wrote the poet W. H. Auden in the 1930s. Today we might say we either cooperate with one another or face a more miserable, brutish existence. Being in the EU obliges that cooperation. Brexit would take Britain backwards.

Recently I read a delightful letter in *The Times* in which a couple declared they would consult their children and grandchildren before casting their vote. They reasoned that as Britain's future mattered more to the next generation than to those of us who have seen out the majority of our days, they, as voters, should take advice or a mandate from those too young to vote but who would be most affected by the decision on 23 June 2016.

Edmund Burke famously wrote that society is based on a contract 'between those who are living, those who are dead, and those who are to be born'. Every time I hear a Brexit isolationist I think of those not yet born who will not enjoy the rights that I have enjoyed as a result of European integration, and the dismantling rather than reinforcing of national protectionism. Every time I think of Europe I see my father marching at the head of a body of men to take another European nation's bullet in his shoulder in the first campaigns of World War II. I see an uncle I never met drowning in the Arctic Convoys as the European nationalisms rose up in war and we had to help our allies at the cost of our nation's young men, one my mother's brother.

They suffered because the power and passion of the nation rose supreme over the compromise and conciliation of a supra-national organization. I don't yet have grandchildren, but I want them and their parents to enjoy all the benefits that ever-closer union in Europe has conferred on me.

That does not make me a blinkered Europhile, a dreamer about impossible forms of post-national governance. I can list more problems with the functioning of the EU than most simply because I know and understand how it works.

I will deal with some of the anti-European arguments in due course. But in the end, if you don't like or want to be in the European Union, no listing of facts will change your mind.

3

UNHAPPY EUROPE

I wrote my 50 reasons to like Europe nearly a decade ago in 2007 and things haven't been looking so good for Europe since. We have seen:

- The financial crash that was so brilliantly portrayed in the movie *The Big Short* (can we finally accept that the crash was imported from America and not made in Britain?) has done and is doing severe economic damage to Europe, driving down growth and driving up unemployment. In Britain we have increased public and private debt and printed money in best Keynesian fashion to deal with the bankers' follies of the Greenspan era. Out-of-date economic ideology from centre-right parties who control the EU Council and Commission and are dominant with other rightists in the European Parliament has prevented adequate responses. So too has determined opposition to necessary reform from vested interests in many countries.

- Mass people movement from the warzones of Iraq, Libya and Syria, all in part the responsibility of European states which used military force to destroy states or encourage civil war, has had no adequate answer from European states. Each has reacted differently – some seeking to be generous but also assuming other states would take a quota of refugees, and others erecting new barriers, putting razor wire on frontier crossings, imposing quotas on how many can transit their territory in search of refuge in richer northern Europe.

- The rise of populist nationalist parties whose leaders seek to win support by decrying the European Union or adopting illiberal measures to control the media or reduce the independence of judges. Until recently the Conservative Party in Britain shared this passion for rubbishing the EU at every opportunity. David Cameron finally appears to have woken up to how full-on political Euroscepticism combined with a plebiscite can lead to a new isolationism.

- The drift of voters to nationalist and populist extremes of both right and left, meaning that it is not possible to elect stable governments in Spain or Ireland, and elsewhere politicians are able to govern only as minority governments or in uneasy coalitions. The quality of leadership in Europe is at its weakest in 70 years.

- The arrival in the European Parliament of scores of MEPs whom Nick Clegg described as 'nutters, anti-Semites and homophobes' means that the confidence of the ordinary citizen in the democratic process of parliamentary supervision and control of EU affairs is much reduced.

- A sense that Brussels is 'too bossy and bureaucratic', to use David Cameron's words. The foreign secretary, Philip Hammond, said in October 2014 that holding the Brexit plebiscite amounted to 'lighting a fire in Europe'. He was pandering to Conservative activists at the Tory Party conference, but as with unending criticism of the EU for its regulations from the CBI, BCC and much of the press we have created an idea of Europe in many minds that is entirely negative.

- Finally there is fear for some and hope for others that a referendum can finally bring an end to Britain's four-decade-long membership of the EU.

Most present-day Conservatives – including David Cameron and those of his ministers who follow his line on voting against Brexit – have spent their political lives espousing the same views as London Mayor Boris Johnson and the Justice Secretary Michael Gove or the former Tory leaders Iain Duncan Smith and Michael Howard, who are campaigning for Brexit. The Prime Minister now says that until he entered Downing Street he did not know the importance of the EU for our prosperity and security. Can he be serious? I took part in just about every Commons debate on Europe between 1997 and 2010 and Mr Cameron was told plenty of times that his and his party's obsessive opposition to Europe was not worthy of a major party hoping to form a government. He now sounds like Tony Blair or Gordon Brown in defending the UK's place in the EU.

But between 1997 and May 2015 he didn't listen. However, there is always room for one more pro-European and I welcome his conversion and wish him well in defeating the isolationist partisans of Brexit.

4

WE ARE ALL SCEPTICS NOW

In fact, every thinking citizen should be sceptical about all those in authority over us. I am sceptical about decisions the UK government makes, about the decisions the London Mayor takes and often sceptical about the administration of the NHS, our schools and the prison system. Does that make me an Anglosceptic or UKsceptic?

In Britain for the past 20 years, the Conservative Party, much of the press and many in the ruling banking and business elites have not expressed a rational scepticism about Europe, but a deeper, visceral and, at times, unpleasant contempt for the muddled and muddied efforts to try and get 28 competing different nations to sink some of their age-old differences and learn to cooperate and even in some areas speak and act as one.

The deal arrived at between Downing Street and Brussels in February 2016 does not, in truth, alter much. That is not to dismiss what has been agreed. It may have the perverse effect of encouraging all other 27 EU member states to go down the same road of threatening a plebiscite unless they get concessions, this time from the UK as well as other EU member states.

The centrifugal forces in Europe are clear enough. In Warsaw and Budapest and Athens and Rome, national leaders get off on slamming the EU. So even as I hope that Britain votes to stay in the EU, that is not enough to save Europe from the threat of regressing to a continent of nationalisms – a disaster, in my view, for our common peace, prosperity and security. So in a sense, defeating the Brexit isolationists, while necessary, is not enough. I do not want Britain just to say 'No' to Brexit but to engage our diplomatic skills, business talent, networks of NGOs, our history of creating and shaping international treaty organizations in being part of a new leadership in Europe to make our region of the world an example of cooperation, tolerance and constant adding value to people's lives.

All the arguments made against the EU – some sharing of power over national law, the cost of membership, regulations that cannot be vetoed by the House of Commons – apply in different measure to the United Nations, the World Trade Organization, the Law of the Sea Treaty, international conventions on refugees, the International Labour Organization and many more supra-national organizations that make judgments and issue rulings we are obliged to obey unless we want to resign from membership.

As the great nineteenth-century Liberal Prime Minister William Gladstone put it, for Britain the 'arbitrament of the court is preferable to the arbitrament of the sword' as he defended some ruling that went against Britain and which was opposed by proud Tories of the day insisting on the supremacy of whatever the House of Commons desired at the time.

Britain should embrace international treaties and support judgments and courts to which we can appeal. For many across the Channel, the European Union has been taken over by the Brits and is today too far simply a free-trade zone devoid of any real political union or purpose. Oh, to see ourselves as others see us! In Paris, Berlin and Brussels the federal dreamers of a fully integrated European Union have given up on their hopes. French politicians and commentators, in particular, argue that the EU has been fashioned by Britain with a weak Brussels and strong national governments. For good or ill, the EU is largely intergovernmental and that is mostly thanks to British efforts. As Jochen Bittner, a German journalist who had been a Brussels correspondent, wrote in the *New York Times* in March 2016, Britain is one of the most influential nations in shaping Europe. 'Churchill liberated Europe. Margaret Thatcher molded it into a single market. Tony Blair enlarged it. Hyperbole or not, there's no doubt Britain played critical roles at the critical moment.'

It seems perverse in the extreme for the UK to walk out of an international treaty organization where we have so much influence and could have even more if we had not wasted the years of this century exploring the interstices of our Eurosceptic navels.

As Wolfgang Schäuble, Germany's finance minister, told the German–British Forum annual conference in London in March 2016: 'I hope Brexit will not happen but if it does it will be very dangerous for the European Union. It would weaken the EU. In British history the UK has always wanted a stable continent. A weaker continental Europe would be a danger for Britain.'

Britain has been grappling for 500 years with the question of Europe. Look at the painting in the National Portrait Gallery of the English and Spanish negotiating teams who drew up the Treaty of London in 1604 after long haggling sessions at Somerset House. They ended the 19-year struggle between Protestant England and Catholic Spain. We didn't win. The Spanish didn't lose. But peace was restored, at least until the next wars came along. I defy anyone to say which are the English negotiators and which the Spanish. (A clue is that there were five on our side and six on their side, as both Spain and the Spanish provinces in the low countries – today's Belgium and Netherlands – had to be represented.)

With the help of the library in the Foreign Office I have held in my hands the original Treaty of Utrecht which ended the Wars of Succession for control of Spain in 1713. It is like a musty paperback, and its 90-odd different clauses – including one that ceded Gibraltar to British rule – read like an eighteenth-century set of EU regulations.

5

AU REVOIR TO SCOTLAND

Jacques Delors said that you cannot fall in love with a single market. He's right. But I think it is perfectly reasonable to love the idea of Europe as much as you love the idea of your own country and the country of your forebears. President Lyndon Johnson's wife said her husband had so much love in him he just had to share it with other women. For me there is no such thing as adulterous patriotism. I can love more than the nation in which I was born, Scotland, and the state I in which grew up and worked, the United Kingdom. I can be proud of being a European citizen without being unfaithful to my British identity.

I leave it to others like Stanley Johnson and his Environmentalists for Europe to make the case that EU rules and support for protecting nature in Britain better help the cause of supporting the countryside than rules made just in Britain.

I leave it to Lord Stuart Rose of the 'Stronger In' campaign to make the economic case, though I might wish the bankers and business leaders had not spent the first 15 years of this century moaning about Europe and finding countless reasons why they thought the EU was a pain in the fundament. How many people have they persuaded into a deep dislike and contempt for the EU over recent years?

I leave it to Peter Mandelson with his double-hat as the UK's former trade minister and the former EU commissioner for trade to explain why the 200,000 British firms which export to Europe might not enjoy being outside the single market which Brexit would entail.

I leave it to the journalist Hugo Dixon and his excellent InFacts team to expose the non-stop untruths from the Brexit propagandists who carry on the tradition of claiming that Europe wants to enforce straight bananas or square tomatoes or fix the size of British condoms.

I leave it to the Conservative activist Peter Wilding of British Influence to explain in his outfit's booklet *Brexit: What Would Happen if the UK Voted to Leave* many of the extremely negative consequences of a 'Leave' decision.

Like the Prime Minister, who has had to declare his previous years of attacks on Europe redundant, they all have only a few weeks to persuade the British people to forget the business and political criticisms of Europe. Instead they are talking about exports, trade, jobs and bread-and-butter arguments.

I hope their new enthusiasm for the EU carries the day. I have never argued that leaving Europe meant apocalypse tomorrow for Britain. We are great, big, mature, economically OK-ish democracy and will continue trading and doing business and respecting most EU rules because they are just common sense.

I think there would be various economic prices to pay and we would become a poorer, meaner nation still dependent on immigrant labour to do all the rotten jobs the white Englishman or -woman won't do. But dear old Britain, or possibly dear old England as Scotland may go its own way, will be still the same.

As someone born in Scotland, with family there and a son who studied at Edinburgh University, I am concerned that Britain walking out of Europe could lead to Scotland walking out of the United Kingdom in order to remain an EU member state.

I find hypocritical the support for European unity from the Scottish nationalists Nicola Sturgeon and Alex Salmond while they simultaneously promote British disunity. Nicola and Alex are closer to Nigel and Boris than to those of us who want to promote union within the British Isles and within Europe. I would prefer Britain to stay in union with Europe and Scotland to stay in union with the rest of Britain.

The forces of nationalist disunity are now genies out of the bottle, but those English dis-uniters who want us out of Europe have no answer if they cede to the Scottish dis-uniters who will then want Scotland out of the UK.

6

OK, SINCE YOU INSIST, A BIT ON ECONOMICS

In 1960, Mexico and Spain had the same per capita GDP, the President of Mexico told Felipe González, then Spanish prime minister, at a conference in the 1990s. Now, Spain has a per capita GDP twice that of Mexico according to the World Bank (US$ 33,838 for Spain; US$ 17,950 for Mexico). Once-poor countries, such as Ireland, Greece and Portugal, have made much bigger advances in national prosperity since they joined the EU than in any comparable period in their history. Ireland has managed a 7.5 per cent growth in her economy in the last 12 months. This is far removed from the poor Ireland before the Emerald Isle entered the European Community. The same is true of Eastern Europe.

One of the great lies of the anti-Europeans is that in the 1975 referendum people voted to join a free-trade area, not a broader union of nations with ambitions beyond creating a common market. This simply isn't true. As Roger Liddle pointed out in his 2015 Policy Network essay *The Risk of Brexit*, in 1975 the government issued a 16-page pamphlet to every voter called *Britain's New Deal in Europe*. It gave five reasons why the Treaty of Rome was signed and why the UK should now vote to remain in the then EEC.

These were:

- to bring together the peoples of Europe
- to raise living standards and improve working conditions
- to promote growth and world trade
- to help the poorer regions of Europe and the rest of world
- to help maintain peace and freedom.

As Liddle drily observes: 'These are ambitious and progressive political objectives for an entity whose only rationale was allegedly the promotion of free trade!' He rightly goes on to point out: 'Yet "we only ever voted to join a common market" is a myth that anti-Europeans over the last three decades have propagated with so much success it is widely believed.'

In the 1975 referendum campaign a poster proclaimed it was better to lose a little sovereignty within Europe than to lose sons on the battlefield. Margaret Thatcher lit a candle for peace as a symbol of European integration in the 1975 campaign. So it really is the most awful nonsense to pretend that 40 years ago the only question was about free trade and a common market.

In fact, too many confuse a single or common market with free trade. A single market means that no government can erect barriers to trade. A British lorry driver can load up his truck with Marmite and Yorkshire Tea and drive from Poland to Portugal, from the Arctic Circle to the Aegean Sea, to hunt for customers. Compare that to the USA and Mexico under the North American Free Trade Agreement (NAFTA). The Mexican trucker can load up with a lorry-load of Corona beer, but once he arrives at the US border, he has to off-load his beer bottles onto an American truck driven by an American trucker.

After mad cow disease, the USA banned all imports of British beef until 2013. The Buy America laws privilege anything bought with taxpayers' dollars to opt for made-in-the-USA products and services. Low-cost airlines cannot fly from the UK to America as they can to Europe. President George W. Bush slapped a tariff on British steel in order to win votes in Pittsburgh and other steel-making states in America to help win the 2000 election. The USA is a great trading nation and imports massively from the UK and from around the world. It believes in free trade but, with just a little bit of political pressure, it can turn protectionist.

Free trade is not the same as a single market. All the protection-ist acts by the USA are impossible under EU rules and laws. After a short period and a temporary ban on British meat exports over legit-imate health scares, the EU accepted that British beef was safe and allowed it to be sold across Europe, while the entire Commonwealth and even the then-UK colony of Hong Kong banned it along with the USA.

Today, Germany takes 50 per cent of all lamb meat exports from the UK. If the UK were outside the EU, it would be easy for Germany to impose a ban, as the health-conscious German meat consumer would insist on no more imports of British meat in the event of an outbreak of foot and mouth, or some other livestock ailment that does not affect the meat but can be whipped up into a health scare leading to a ban.

In his letter sent in February 2016 to EU member state gov-ernments about Brexit, the EU Council President, Donald Tusk, stressed the need for more competitiveness:

> The European Council highlights the enormous value of the internal market as an area without frontiers within which goods, persons, services and capital move unhindered. This constitutes one of the Union's greatest achievements. In these times of eco-nomic and social challenges, we need to breathe new life into the internal market and adapt it to keep pace with our changing environment. Europe must boost its international competive-ness across the board in services and products and in key areas such as energy and the digital single market.

These fine words about the 'need to breathe new life into the internal market' for services and products 'and in key areas such as energy and the digital single market' – which even some pro-Brexit people support – mean one thing. For these ambitions to be realized there will have to be more, not less Europe. There will have to be more EU-wide regulations and laws to break or wear down the national protectionisms that still exist.

Each country, for example, has its own approach to energy. In Britain, we imposed very high charges on users of electricity in order to meet carbon reduction targets. The sharp rise in electricity prices has had enormous consequences for industries like steel, glass and paper, which need a huge amount of heat at key moments in the production process. None of the Conservative or Liberal Democrat ministers after 2010 who imposed these charges had any direct knowledge of industrial production.

They managed to do almost terminal damage, especially to the UK steel industry. In Poland, by contrast, the government of whatever political colour remains wedded to burning brown coal (lignite), the most polluting of any coal dug up and burnt.

To get a common EU energy policy, it will be necessary to bring together Polish and British approaches. The point is not to say one is right and the other wrong, but simply to point out that someone, somewhere has to set the rules and that means more power, not less, for the EU.

Decisions will be taken by majority vote, but in some energy sectors such majority-vote decisions will not be popular. The same is true for the idea of creating a single market for digital economy users. And don't mention the Capital Markets Union, which the UK's member of the European Commission, Lord Jonathan Hill, is meant to bring into being. This means the banks, savings firms, insurance companies, pension funds and other bodies to which we entrust our money to be lent out as capital all operate under one single set of rules.

Rules to protect our money, savings, pensions or insurance schemes have been at the heart of national legislation for more than a century, if not longer. It will be impossible to create a capital markets union, or complete the internal market in services, or have a digital economy union without new rules being set.

Thus it's sheer hypocrisy to condemn the EU for its rule setting, while simultaneously demanding that it sets ever more common rules to force through the abolition of national protectionisms.

We either have each nation state and each parliament insisting it has the democratic right and national duty to uphold national traditions and laws, even if these are protectionist and a barrier to trade and our right to live freely in other EU nations, or we have a single market and free movement. It is impossible to have both.

7

BREXIT INTERRUPTUS

Most defences of Europe are written in a pained tone. 'The EU is good for you', is the line, a bit like the Syrup of Figs poured down children's throats to make sure they were 'regular'. Defenders of Europe have to nervously cough, and spend half their time explaining that, yes, yes, there are lots of problems, and yes, yes, it's imperfect, but if you look at it all a bit more deeply you will come to realize, that on balance, just about, taking one thing with another, maybe it's better not to risk leaving.

Or they say, let's stay in Europe but please not this Europe, but the Europe of our hopes, dreams, desires. These can be for a more aggressive capitalist ultra-liberal Europe, maybe for a greener wind-power Europe, perhaps for a tough military Europe able to stand up to the Kremlin's foreign policy adventures and patrol its closed frontiers to repel political and economic refugees, or for a more social, pro-worker, trade-union-friendly Europe.

But the commentaries on Europe are often a long dirge, with even nominal pro-Europeans having to bang on and on about all the faults they can find in the EU before grudgingly admitting they aren't in favour of leaving.

It makes being in the EU sound like a sour, loveless, childless marriage, with virile Britain aching for adventures new but unable to be bold and brave and stop fretting about the money and go out and be a MAN and dump the old thing some past nuptial treaty has forced us to live with for too many miserable years.

Some, of course, are nervous of taking their Brexit testosterone urges to full consummation. They prefer *Brexit interruptus*, putting off withdrawal as long as possible. The cerebral Conservative minister Oliver Letwin is reported to have told his colleagues not to worry about Brexit in 2016. Instead they should wait for the next EU Treaty negotiation. Then London can make demands that cannot be met, and hey presto, Brexit happens without effort. The rising Tory cabinet minister Sajid Javid is a prime example of the *Brexit interruptus* politician. He has lined up behind the Prime Minister but done so with grudging grumpiness, saying that Britain would, in the long term, be better off outside the EU and he would never have supported entry in the first place.

So David Cameron has to reply on these supporters of Brexit – but not this year – to enthuse the voting public into a 'Yes' or 'Remain'.

Boris Johnson, on the other hand, has refused to turn his coat. A life-long fabulator about the European Union in general and a Savonarola about the European Commission in particular, for Boris being anti-European was all part of a political virility based on an enduring antipathy to Europe and a sturdy refusal expressed in wonderfully polemical speeches and articles to be entrapped or seduced by any of the wiles and tricks that Europe can invent.

And it's true, Europe is the feminine gender of politics so the *Boy's Own* Boris, MP for Swagger and Masculinity East, has never really fitted in. Europe is slippery subjunctives expressing wishes, longing, uncertainty, not the manly assertiveness of a politics that knows no doubt.

It is literally feminine in other languages. '*Die* europäische Union', '*une* union toujours plus étroite', to quote from the Treaty preamble. These are warm female nouns, with the Union's defining word *européenne* softening, rounding the noun. The more I think of it, the more the Europhobes are macho-posturing, cocky, self-centred domineering males – Nigel Farage, Geert Wilders or Jean-Marie Le Pen.

PART TWO

8
IT'S GEO-POLITICS, STUPID

It's the non-economic facts, the geo-political changes in my country's status and ability to do good in the world, that concern me. Russia's strongman Vladimir Putin has a very simple foreign policy. It is: 'Russia UP. America DOWN. Europe OUT.'

Brexit would be a major win for Putin's worldview, which rejects any international cooperation or common rules and believes that the only actors in world or European affairs should be nation states. If you are a unitary centralized state run from one building, the Kremlin, in one city, Moscow, that might make sense. But Russia has invaded and semi-annexed part of a European nation state, Georgia, and annexed a chunk of another UN member state in Europe, namely in Ukraine.

To be sure, smarter Western diplomacy in the 1990s and a US president other than George W. Bush after 2001 might have made a difference. But Russia refuses to cooperate with the EU as a whole. As in past moments of Russian history Western-orientated pro-Europeans in Moscow seem to have been sidelined by traditional Russian Slavists who want control over their immediate neighbourhood, as the Kremlin prods and provokes Poland and the Baltic States and uses aggressive language followed up by over-flights aimed at EU Nordic member states.

Britain walking out of Europe would confirm Russia in its wish to see a Balkanized Europe of nation states coming apart instead of a Europe from Galway to European Russia becoming more and more united to promote liberal economic rule-of-law values as well as those of an open democracy and open society.

Brexit is no answer to the threat from Islamist ideology that fuels hate against the democratic values of Europe to the extent of turning young men into terrorists. Britain is not in the Schengen zone, but this did not stop the 7/7 London bombings in 2005. The Madrid Atocha bombings in 2004 had nothing to do with free movement. Irish nationalists or Marxist groups exploded bombs killing people in England and Italy in the 1970s, and the Basque ETA terrorists did the same in the 1980s, well before Schengen passport-free travel was created. It is good policing, good intelligence sharing, the speedy rendering of terrorists using the European Arrest Warrant and an understanding of the ideological roots of radicalization that will defeat the most recent terrorism that has struck Paris and Brussels and may strike again. The biggest win for Islamist terror would be to respond by closing frontiers. Defeating terror requires more European cooperation and common security, police and judicial cooperation.

When I was a student at Oxford during the 1968 upheavals, a fully democratic Europe was limited to a handful of countries. Even in France, General de Gaulle decided what the main headlines should be in the evening TV news. Ireland and Italy were under the thumb of the Catholic Church. Germany did not allow left-ists to work in the public service. Greece, Spain and Portugal were dictatorships. Half of Europe lay under communist control, with key policies dictated by the Soviet Union and freedom of expression crushed.

Half a century later, Europe is utterly different. Of course there are imperfections. Democracy is now flourishing in 28 EU member states and democratic elections sometimes throw up results that are not to my taste. I would prefer Poland and Hungary not to have such illiberal governments. But that for the time being is the choice of their electorates, and it is up to more progressive political parties to develop policies and find leaders who can appeal to a majority – a problem that my own party, Labour, now has to deal with.

When Paris was liberated by the Free French Army in 1944, General de Gaulle said 'From one day to the next, the people of Paris could say what they liked, meet who they wanted, go where they desired.' As a working definition of democratic freedom de Gaulle's isn't bad, even if he wasn't exactly a stellar liberal as President of France, 1958–1969.

I remember sitting in fear in a communist prison in Warsaw in 1982 after being arrested while taking money to the underground trade union Solidarity. I wondered then if ever the day would come when Poles could say what they liked, meet who they wanted and go where they wished. It came to pass as the magnetic attraction of Europe helped to push communist governments into the dustbin of history. But who of my children's generation (born in the '80s and '90s) knows anything of communism or what a Europe divided up into blocs and rival nation states was like? Today those broad conditions of freedom now exist all over the 28 member states of the EU.

There is another vital European body, the Council of Europe, set up upon the urging of Winston Churchill, which also upholds these broad freedoms. But unlike the EU, the Council of Europe has no enforceable powers and only limited jurisdiction via the European Court of Human Rights. This means that countries like Russia, Azerbaijan and Turkey, where there are serious limits on political democracy and freedom of expression and harassment of journalists is the norm, are in the Council of Europe but nothing can be done to get these states to abide by Council of Europe rules.

In the EU there is an assumption that governments will seek to be full democracies. For Greece, then Spain and Portugal, joining with other member states of the European Community enshrined their status and their obligations as full members of the democratic community of nations. When the ex-communist Soviet bloc states entered the European Union the same happened.

There is an argument that the EU is turning its back on democracy promotion to focus only on economic and single-market priorities. To a certain extent, citizens in a country unhappy at new rulers who seek to meddle in media and judicial affairs sometimes demand that the EU intervenes on their behalf. But the EU cannot substitute itself for a failure of internal politics. To be sure, if the new political rulers of an EU member state are egregious or blatant in breaching democratic norms there are mechanisms to allow reprimand, even intervention, as there are at the Council of Europe. At some stage the EU may have to suspend or boot out a member state that egregiously violates Europe's democratic norms. It would be no bad thing, *pour encourager les autres* as Voltaire put it.

But so far the EU has been the best democracy promoter ever seen in the history of Europe. Of course, Britain outside of Europe will remain a vigorous democracy. Our free media, free Parliament and rule-of-law traditions are deep-rooted. But it would send every wrong signal to those less enthusiastic about liberal democracy for the UK to walk out of the common union of nations we all belong to.

This is why I think Europe is important and why I believe that if European union (with a small or big 'u') weakens or becomes smaller we will be the losers. So this is a statement of emotional identity.

It is almost impossible to overstate the impact of Brexit on global affairs. At a stroke, the status and authority of Europe as an actor in the Middle East, with Iran, in relation to China and India would be seriously diminished, if indeed it did not disappear. British global experience in terms of hard and soft power, in terms of the experience and abilities of British diplomats and international officials would no longer be united with European partners.

When I was Europe minister every month I would fly with the Foreign Secretary or sometimes alone with some able British public servants for a meeting with foreign ministers from 27 other countries. It was a chance to argue for and insist on British priorities like the handing over of Balkan war criminals to an international tribunal or getting a travel ban imposed on the tyrant of Zimbabwe, Robert Mugabe. But it was also a moment to listen to the priorities of countries such as Cyprus or Estonia which otherwise don't get much of a hearing in global fora. I could arrange joint visits with my French or German opposite number and have private talks in Spanish with ministers from Madrid to try and get some easing of frontier problems with Gibraltar.

The terrible Balkans conflicts unleashed by the Serb leader Slobodan Milošević or the later oppression of the Albanian minority in Macedonia were able to be resolved, in part, thanks to this regular contact and cooperation between elected politicians and their officials from all EU member states.

To deny Britain that possibility as a result of Brexit will be to do serious damage to the UK's ability to influence European and world affairs.

Without Britain, Germany will be the overwhelmingly dominant power in the EU, perhaps seeking to have military power, including nuclear weapons, concomitant with its economic weight.

It is hard to seeing the so-called special relationship with America surviving a decision to isolate Britain from Europe. The EU needs to find solutions to the problems of poverty, lack of investment and political authoritarianism in its immediate neighbours across the Mediterranean in Morocco, Tunisia, Algeria and Egypt, as well as restore some stability to Libya.

Minus Britain this will be harder to achieve. There is safety in numbers and in agreeing a common line on how to handle a major world problem like the threat from Islamist violence or supporting democracy campaigners in Burma and elsewhere.

A go-it-alone Britain at odds with its European sister nations will make the world a less stable, possibly, indeed probably, a more dangerous place.

9

NATIONS DON'T RUN ON STRAIGHT LINES, NOR DOES EUROPE

The EU is a family of nations, full of the conflicts, disagreements, walk-outs, sulks and shouting matches that every family knows. But, as we all know, it's family that makes the world go around. Families are messy compromises where the strong are asked to help the weak, where the clever gently educate the stupid, the rule-breakers are chastised, where those with more cash quietly lend some money to those not so smart in managing budgets and where sins are forgiven.

'Out of the crooked timber of humanity', wrote the philosopher Immanuel Kant, 'no straight thing was ever made.' The same is true of European construction. Eurosceptics are always complaining that they have to obey rules in order to be part of the EU.

They protest that they cannot opt out of a directive or policy every time they don't like what is decided. They never point out that directives are agreed by democratically elected ministers from 28 different parliaments and governments.

Certainly the European Commission proposes and drafts the directive with the approval of ministers sent from London, Rome, Berlin, Dublin and other capitals. I know because I had to put my hand up to agree EU decisions when I was a minister. I observed close up how the prime minister, with very smart, patriotic British officials in attendance, chews over every vote and seeks allies in order to ensure Britain's interests are upheld. Nothing the EU does happens without agreement from a majority of democratically elected governments.

Most decisions need an added layer of democratic protection to be approved by the European Parliament, where democratically elected British MEPs have a voice and a vote. I think national parliaments should be more directly involved in partnership with MEPs in the democratic oversight of what the EU does. If one day the EU does set about reforming the way it does business, a new foundation for the EU should seek positive rather than passive consent to what it is and what it does from its citizens. The best way to do this is to associate national parliaments with European decisions by creating a second chamber of the European Parliament, a kind of Senate drawn from national parliaments. Another mechanism might be to have elections for MEPs at the same time as national elections so that MEPs represent the political choice of their national parliaments.

Thanks to Margaret Thatcher, all EU member states, under pressure from her, agreed to give up vetoes in some important areas. That meant that a single state could not block all the others from going forward with a measure they thought necessary. It is why those on the left who support the EU consider Mrs Thatcher to be our best European prime minister in terms of allowing Britain to have a voice and a vote through the mechanism of majority votes that allowed so many barriers to be dismantled. Mrs Thatcher insisted this was necessary to help remove protectionist barriers and allow British people, British goods, British firms, British service industries like banking and insurance and law firms, to work anywhere in Europe. She was right to make that case in the 1980s and legislate what is called the Single European Act, which was a major new EU Treaty, in many ways the most important one since the founding Treaty of Rome.

Margaret Thatcher was notorious for being a proud manager of a household. She understood that one must set certain basic rules to allow a family whose members are at different stages of maturity and development to live in some harmony, despite the competing needs and wishes of different family members.

Thanks to the EU, every man and woman knows that we live in a region of the world where the casual gun violence that kills 88 Americans every day is simply not tolerated. Mothers know that if their sons or daughters have an accident anywhere in the EU, there is free emergency hospital treatment and care without having to hand over a credit card, as in the rest of the world.

This feminine European Union will accept a son or daughter who is gay without hanging them from a crane as in Iran, or stoning them to death in countries where unreformed religious violence still holds sway, especially over the lives of young women.

Of course, if the elderly, macho, failed-marriage males who proclaim their Europhobia from every platform, radio studio or comment column get their way, Britain will not turn into an anti-woman nation. But the criss-cross mesh of EU laws, directives and obligations to respect the EU's and the Council of Europe's main conventions that protect women constitute one of the most significant feminist advances in history. Amongst there are:

- equal economic independence for women and men
- equal pay for work of equal value
- equality in decision-making
- dignity, integrity and ending gender violence
- promoting gender equality beyond the EU.

Certainly there are declarations by the United Nations and such agencies as the International Labour Organization or the World Health Organization which seek to protect women. But they are not enforceable and have limited legal authority. What the all-male Eurosceptics dislike is that the EU and European Court of Human Rights (linked to the Council of Europe) impose enforceable obligations on states to protect and support women. History does not move forward on its own. The advances made in the field of women's rights since the 1950s have required enormous campaigning effort by European women.

To deny British women that protection, to remove, dilute or weaken those rights seems foolish and unwise.

10

NO MORE WAR

We tend to cringe when the claim is made that European integration has ended war in Europe. For a start, it hasn't. There were the foul Balkans wars initiated by the Serb strongman Slobodan Milošević in the 1990s. These culminated in the Katyn-style massacre of 8,000 unarmed Europeans taken prisoner by the Serbs and put to death in cold blood at Srebrenica in 1995. Britain led the campaign to stop Milošević's second genocidal attack – this time on Kosovans in 1998, when 850,000 had to flee their country to stop Serb killing squads running amok. Nor has Europe stopped Vladimir Putin from dismembering Georgia in 2008 or feeding an irregular war against the government of Ukraine from its eastern Donbass regime, which the Kremlin regards as being under Russian dominance.

There have been ugly little conflicts involving the IRA or ETA in the Basque country, which have required a militarized security response. French President François Hollande said that France was 'at war' after the Islamist slaughter in Paris in November 2015, but like President George W. Bush's 'war on terror' after 9/11, the struggle against Jihadi Islamist ideology and its killers is not armed conflict between states.

Instead, Europe has enjoyed the most peaceful 70 years of existence in the last two millennia. It is astonishing that my parents' generation and their parents' generation who had known the great wars of the first half of the twentieth century were able to see their children and grandchildren in every country in Europe grow up and flourish without the shadow of war.

In the seventeenth, eighteenth, nineteenth and twentieth centuries, Britain had to send its sons to die in land wars on the continent or naval engagements in the seas around Europe to protect British interests. Blood and treasure was expended to stop any dominant force rising on the European continent – a powerful nation, an arrogant religion, an antipathetic ideology – that might threaten Britain's peace or its core commercial interests.

European integration and the intertwining of Britain with Europe through commerce, open borders and the right of any British citizen to open a business or live anywhere in Europe has surely reduced to zero any chance of an existential threat from across the Channel. US President General Dwight D. Eisenhower found it hard to believe that the warring nations of Europe, which twice required the arrival of US armies to defeat evil, could finally lay their demons to rest. At US National Security Council meetings in the 1950s, President Eisenhower encouraged his cabinet to speak both privately and in public in favour of European integration. And contrary to the myth that the 1957 Treaty of Rome was just about trade and a common market, Washington supported political union in Europe. As Henry Kissinger has written:

> As late as 1962, Under Secretary of State Ball warned against the danger of treating the Common Market simply as an economic enterprise and opposed efforts of the Scandinavian countries and Austria to enter it without making a commitment to political unity.

US presidents after 1945 have been on their knees begging Britain and other EU nations to keep integrating and ensuring that open borders, free trade, free movement and enforceable rules make the concept of conflict again arising between European nations unthinkable.

To be sure, NATO, the great military alliance put in place by the Labour government after 1945, has been vital. But NATO without the EEC, today the EU, would have remained a thin alliance of armies unable, for example, to prevent Turkey invading Cyprus and annexing the northern third of the island in 1974. NATO was unable to roll back Soviet communist rule in Eastern Europe. NATO never opened a market or allowed low-cost airlines to land anywhere in Europe, as the officials of the much-maligned Brussels European civil service did when they broke up national airline cartels that made air travel something only the rich enjoyed when I was my children's age.

Instead, the magnetic attraction to Poles, Czechs, Hungarians and Slovenians of the shining example of economic and cultural and citizen freedom in the integrated Europe built by Jacques Delors, Margaret Thatcher, François Mitterrand and Helmut Kohl in the 1980s was the key element that helped bury communism.

So let's hang on to NATO, which also involves a fair degree of sharing sovereignty, accepting orders from foreign generals and, in its Article 5, an absolute obligation to go to war with any nation that attacks a NATO member – a far greater derogation of national sovereignty than anything in EU Treaties, as Professor Peter Hennessy has pointed out – but do not let the isolationists say Europe is not about war and peace.

The dead on the beaches of Normandy, at Arnhem, on the slopes of Monte Casino or the British, Polish and Czech pilots who gave their lives to save Britain from Nazism in 1940 will cry from their graves: 'Never again the Europe of the nation *über Alles*. Protect and cherish the Europe we could never enjoy as foolish politicians believed what happened on the continent had nothing to do with the off-shore European island of Great Britain!'

In February 2016, the United States announced that it was increasing fourfold its military expenditure in Europe. This is mainly in response to Vladimir Putin's remilitarization of Russia, something that deeply worries Eastern European and Baltic State EU members. The geo-political consequences of a Brexit vote would be grave indeed. The Euro-Atlantic partnership of the USA and the EU, combined with NATO, has been a major contributor to a better

world in my lifetime. Even when its component parts make mis-
takes, such as the military interventions in Iraq and Libya, or the
unnecessary sacrifice of 500 British soldiers' lives in Afghanistan after
2010 because Prime Minister Cameron did not know how to win
back control of the war there from his generals, the Euro-Atlantic
democracies are self-correcting. Wantonly breaking away from the
rest of Europe would be a disastrous signal to send to America
and other friends like Canada and Australia with whom the UK
has warm defence and security relationships. That is why leaders in
Canada, Australia and other Commonwealth nations are urging us
to say 'No' to Brexit. They want their friend and founding nation
of the Commonwealth, Great Britain, to have a place at the table in
Brussels where decisions are taken on trade, aid and foreign policy
that affect all Commonwealth member states.

The military balance of power in the Asia-Pacific region is delicate
in the extreme and an act of self-inflicted British isolationism would
send every sort of wrong signal around the world.

11

EUROPE IS MORE THAN POLITICS, BUT POLITICS MATTER

I am a political animal. I first stood for Parliament in 1974. I worked with underground or opposition trade union movements in Poland, Brazil, South Africa and South Korea in the 1980s before becoming an MP in 1994. After 2000 I was Europe minister and then UK delegate to the Council of Europe. I represented the Labour Party on the Party of European Socialists. MPs all have their passions, and Europe was mine.

I welcome the idea that if a majority of EU parliaments oppose a draft law or directive from Brussels it can be stopped. In reality, no proposal that met such a level of hostility from more than half of the EU would stand any chance of becoming EU law. But if that encourages the House of Commons to take the EU seriously, to work and form committees with parliamentarians from the other 27 EU national parliaments, that is welcome.

However, one of David Cameron's first acts on becoming prime minister was to abolish the full-day debate held before each EU Council meeting which allowed MPs to examine and discuss developments in the EU. If now he is ready to place the Commons at the heart of the UK's relationship with Europe and encourage MPs to take an active interest in what the EU does with proper backing in terms of resources and expenses, this would be a welcome development.

But Europe is more than politics. It's an idea that is so simple and so important that it demands an emotional commitment, a desire to create something bigger and better than the mean-spirited little political cottage that we are supposed to live in.

We don't do the vision thing in British political discourse. We pride ourselves on being pragmatic and results-orientated and like to avoid big definitions.

Sometimes a politician can break out, as when David Cameron told his party to grow up about being gay. 'I don't support gay marriage in spite of being a Conservative. I support gay marriage because I am a Conservative', he declared and in one glorious phrase buried the decades of legalized, judge-enforced Tory homophobia that destroyed so many lives.

That was a simple statement, a vision about fair treatment of gays, not hedged by calculation or bottom-line political ratiocination. Cameron did something similar early in 2016 when he denounced the contemptible failure of the dons, DPhils and gowned dignitaries who run Oxford to find space for black British students. The Prime Minister denounced what he called the 'ingrained, institutional and insidious' attitudes in our top universities towards British students who are not white.

It's the way I feel about Europe. Europhobia, Eurocynicism, Eurosneering, Eurobashing, Eurotrashing, Euroknocking, Eurofatigue, Euromoaning, Euronegativity are modish, available in all our best newspapers, on the *Today* programme or most BBC TV current affairs programmes, easy to overhear in pubs and clubs. The cumulative effect can so easily overwhelm.

When I stood up in the Commons to speak in any EU debate, there was an audible hiss and buzz of anger that anyone should defy the conventional twenty-first-century wisdom that Europe was bad for Britain.

There was a right-wing New Zealander Tory MP, a dentist who gave me good advice on root canal work, but as a fanatically anti-European Tory he would hiss and boo with others whenever I got up to speak on Europe from the Labour benches.

I loved it. The worse thing for an MP is complete indifference when on your feet in the Chamber. Being jeered at by Tory Europhobes gave me a perfect start as I waited, arms folded, for them to quieten down, or they were called to order by the Speaker.

If truth be told, I have never been able to work out the reasons for the passionate opposition to European construction from so many that has been such a constant of my adult life.

12

LABOUR CAN BE AS WRONG AS THE TORIES ON EUROPE

The legendary postwar Labour leader, Hugh Gaitskell, said that to sign the 1957 Treaty of Rome would 'mean the end of Britain as an independent nation state... the end of a thousand years of history.' This hyperbole was silly then, and since signing the Treaty of Rome Britain has gone its own way, launched its own wars in the Falklands or Iraq, has its own taxation and criminal justice policy, changed lots of laws from gay rights to university tuition fees and done so as an independent nation despite Gaitskell's absurd claim.

Here is a president of the Oxford Union, a figure as revered on the Labour left as Gaitskell was on the Labour right. Michael Foot could outdo a Nigel Farage or a Bill Cash with his denunciations of Europe. He told MPs soon after Britain entered the European Economic Community: 'The British parliamentary system has been made farcical and unworkable by the superimposition of the EEC apparatus. It as if we had set fire to the place [the House of Commons] as Hitler did with the Reichstag.' I loved Michael Foot but what on earth possessed this cultured, educated European to make such fatuous statements?

The voters who decide the British parliamentary system weren't very interested in Hugh Gaitskell or Michael Foot, because, despite their brilliant oratory, charm, and capacity for winning friends and followers, the two Labour leaders were better at losing than winning elections. (Michael Foot kindly launched a biography of François Mitterrand I wrote in 1982 but puzzled guests at the launch by saying that, while he was delighted a fellow socialist was now President of France, he could not understand why Mitterrand was so keen on Europe!)

Labour spent much of the 1960s, 1970s and 1980s where the Conservatives are now. The Labour Prime Minister Harold Wilson, like his Conservative successor David Cameron, supported the UK being in Europe but many Labour MPs and ministers and probably a majority of party activists remained hostile.

It was argued that the 1975 referendum would drain the anti-European bile from British politics. The opposite happened. Within a few years the Labour Party's official policy was withdrawal from the European Community. So much for the argument that a referendum, to use Sir John Major's words in March 2013 in praise of Cameron's Brexit plebiscite, 'could heal many old sores and have a cleansing effect on politics'. The idea of a referendum as a political enema may appeal to Sir John, but so far in 2016 there is no evidence of any healing effect from the Cameron plebiscite – at least for Conservative MPs and activists.

The anti-European language of Gaitskell and Foot was lurid and exaggerated. Fast forward to our time, and dear old Boris Johnson writes a biography of Winston Churchill in which all the qualities he discovers in the great Briton – fluent speaker, a way with the written word, controversialist, erratic political loyalties, tremendous eater and drinker, non-stop self-publicism, disliked by many in his party – all these aspects of Winston Churchill's character, no doubt by coincidence, bear a close resemblance to Boris himself. But the Tory Party's No. 1 Eurosceptic outdoes Gaitskell and Foot when he writes of a 'Gestapo-controlled Nazi EU'. It is the kind of game sub-editors invent to while away a boring afternoon before the news starts flowing in: 'Go on, who can get Nazi, Gestapo and EU into a four-word phrase, not even a sentence?!'

Step forward, Boris. It shows his utter unsuitability for high office (mind you, they said the same of Churchill), but today there is not a nation in Europe that wishes ill to our country. Our enemies, if such they may be named, are those filthy anti-democracies – gay-executing, women-covering, journalist-flogging, writer-exiling negations of humanity – where wealth by the billion flows into the pockets of leaders, their families and cronies. But for Boris, as for Hugh and Michael, it is Europe we must reject and oppose.

Chuck it, Johnson. As I write there was a delicious tale that David Cameron, Boris's Eton contemporary but a hundred times more cunning and ruthless, was thinking of seeking to bribe the MP mayor into the 'Remain' campaign by offering him the post of foreign secretary. If true, it did not work as the battle of Bullingdon is now enjoined between these two Old Etonians, members of the Bullingdon Club at Oxford and rivals ever since as they sought to climb the greasy pole of political power, Cameron with more success than Johnson – to date.

Of course if Brexit happens, Cameron will have to resign as it will be the greatest humiliation of a prime minister for more than a century. Johnson will most likely take over in the event of Brexit.

If Brexit is rejected, Boris is still in a good position as the man who stood true to his anti-EU beliefs, and will be seen as the man who represented the Tory rank and file as well as many ministers and MPs who dislike the EU.

The foreign secretary position is not one for Boris. I worked closely as parliamentary private secretary and minister with two foreign secretaries and saw others in action. It is the grandest title in Whitehall but a job empty of substance: anything foreign that matters is dealt with in 10 Downing Street.

The Foreign Office's diplomats remain the smartest and certainly the smoothest in government service, but they know where power lies and make sure their best and brightest are seconded to Downing

Street or the Cabinet Office to steer the Prime Minister and the nation's decisions in the direction that the collective wisdom of the deep state decides is best.

At a grand party early in 2016, a clever permanent secretary friend was leaving and I said I was worried about Brexit. 'Don't worry, Denis. Jeremy has got it all organized.' The Jeremy in question is not the leader of the Opposition but Sir Jeremy Heywood, the head of the Cabinet Office and Civil Service and the fixer-in-chief of the British state Establishment. He is indeed a smart and very personable man with no side and a real sense of public service. But he cannot fix this referendum and would be foolish to think he can.

Indeed, that is why the commanding officials of Whitehall have been so rattled by David Cameron's Brexit plebiscite. The high officials of state can handle ministers, manipulate Parliament, square the press, but a referendum isn't part of the FCO code book. The one in 1975 was easy. Every CEO, every editor, the Prime Minister, the Leader of the Opposition, the entire Establishment, left and right, north and south was in favour.

We had only been in the EEC five minutes. There was no time to get worked up about its directives and laws. No one knew what the European budget was and whether it had been fully audited or not. In 1975 there wasn't a directly elected European Parliament. We were denied the thrill of Nigel Farage and Nick Griffin elected in a proportional representation system: they would never have become MPs by winning votes in distinct, limited constituencies, rather than relying on being top of a party-controlled list of candidates.

To compare the 1975 referendum with Cameron's Brexit plebiscite is simply wrong. It would be better if those who argue that 2016 is a rerun of 1975 parked their comparison.

From my experience as a parliamentary private secretary and minister 1997–2005, the Foreign Office prefers its foreign secretaries to speak or read no foreign languages, never to have worked abroad and to have zero foreign policy experience. That is why they get on so well with the present incumbent.

To begin with I hoped Cameron would offer the bribe and that Boris, in his vanity, would accept. The alternative we now have of Boris as Mr Brexit, putting his undoubted energy and ability into winning a 'Leave' vote in the referendum is worrying, though his early outings on Andrew Marr's BBC TV show displayed acres of mumbling and unproven assertions plus the weird claim we do not have to get visas via the ESTA scheme to travel to America. Boris has US citizenship as he was born there so can travel on a US passport. But the rest of us have to fill in a form (which can be rejected, as with any visa application) and pay money to visit America, which if it became the norm for travel to Europe in the event of Brexit would not be welcome.

Johnson, I repeat, would most probably inherit the crown, because if David Cameron's plebiscite results in an 'Out' vote, then out goes the Prime Minister to enter the special British political Valhalla of shame reserved for prime ministers like Lords North and Aberdeen or Neville Chamberlain or Anthony Eden, who isolated their country from common sense and diminished its standing in the world with damaging consequences.

But to paraphrase Cameron, I don't support the EU in spite of being British. I support the EU because I am British.

US Senator Daniel Moynihan once observed that everyone 'is entitled to his own opinions but not to his own facts'. The Europe debate is opinion-rich and fact-poor. To reverse C.P. Scott's dictum on Europe: 'Comment is sacred. Facts are free.'

Once when campaigning in a general election in South Yorkshire I was stopped by a voter who asked me my views on Europe. I began explaining but before two words were out, he interrupted: 'Denis, stop talking and try listening. You like Europe.'

I began again and at once was cut off: 'No, no, you're talking like all those politicians. I've seen you on TV, I've heard you on radio. You think we should be in Europe, Denis. But we're Yorkshire. We don't want to be in Europe.'

He paused for breath, which allowed me to cut in and say: 'If you mean by being in Europe, the EU or the EEC, we have been in it for 40 years.'

He looked puzzled, paused to think and then said: 'Oh, have we? They don't give us the facts any more, do they?'

No, they certainly do not. If there is one thing that decades of grass-roots, door-to-door, street-level contacts with voters have taught me it is that relying on our media to gain factual information about Europe leaves the voter full of prejudice but devoid of facts. We shall see if by its end the Brexit referendum campaign allows some facts to emerge. On the evidence so far it seems unlikely.

Another problem is the failure to allow nearly 3 million British citizens to take part in the referendum. The Electoral Commission, which is meant to be the ring-holder for our giant ballot-box decisions, is surely the most spectacularly useless quango ever invented.

In response to media reports about electoral fraud – always a problem at the margins of mainly local elections – the Electoral Commission has made it much harder to register to vote. As a result 800,000 mainly young people have been removed from the electoral register so they do not have the right to vote. Young voters are far more likely to vote for Europe than older, more Eurosceptic voters, so the Electoral Commission has made it very difficult for younger voters to take part in a decision on their future. A further 2 million Brits who live in Europe, and might feel that a decision to take away their right of automatic residence, travel, study, work and emergency hospital treatment concerns them as British passport holders, will also be denied a vote.

The reason is that the rules imposed by the Electoral Commission govern an electoral system based on electing candidates for local or national offices from individual constituencies. If you live abroad you remain a British citizen and if you live in Europe the loss of European citizenship and the right to live anywhere in the EU will be devastating. But unless you have kept a home in Britain and renewed your voting registration you lose the right to vote. The Brexit referendum is not based on constituencies or electing anyone. Every British passport holder should be given the right to vote, especially those most directly affected, who live or have retired to different countries in the EU.

Meanwhile, 400,000 citizens of a foreign republic, Irish passport holders living in Britain, can vote as can EU citizens from Malta and Cyprus on the grounds that they are in the Commonwealth. Altogether 1.6 million foreigners can vote on whether we stay in Europe or not. Meanwhile the Brits who live in Spain, work in Berlin, have retired to France or set up a business in Poland and whose future depends on the outcome of the Brexit referendum won't be able to have a say.

I wonder what we will say if Mr Cameron's plebiscite is lost – or won – thanks to Irish or Cypriot votes? He can do the explaining after the event, though if we quit Europe it will be a different prime minister who has to unravel the mess.

There are many good books going through the pros and cons of Britain's membership of the EU. David Charter, former Brussels correspondent of *The Times*, now the paper's Berlin correspondent, has written *Europe: In or Out?* (Biteback). Other books have been written by such journalists and political writers as Hugo Dixon, Lords Roger Liddle and Anthony Giddens, or the Conservative politician John Redwood, whose 1999 book *The Death of Britain?* (Palgrave Macmillan) is a sturdy exposition of the isolationist Brexit case.

Yet with each passing, shuddering wave of events making the good ship Europe tremble and list and seem to be on the point of capsizing, I am more, not less, seized of the importance of the idea of Europe and more strong in my hope that my children and, if they have children, my grandchildren can live in a twenty-first-century Europe that can stay united instead of breaking apart into component rival nationalisms.

The phrase 'ever-closer union among the peoples of Europe' is in the preamble to the Treaty of Rome signed in 1957. Let us note in passing that it does not call for an ever-closer union of states. I like the idea of closer union with other peoples. The opposite doesn't feel too good.

Like the wonderful expression in the American constitution about 'life, liberty and the pursuit of happiness' – a noble aim that failed to prevent a civil war, slavery, continuing racism and grotesque inequalities today, as well as other woes that plague the glorious United States of America – the promise of an ever-closer union of peoples has yet to be realized on our old continent.

It is in the preamble so doesn't have legal weight. In fact, when I was minister for Europe British officials helped remove the term from the EU Treaty that was voted down by the French and the Dutch in 2005. It was grandly called a Constitution but in fact was just another of the many European integration treaties that have been produced since 1950, and especially since 1957, to allow a common set of rules, which all must obey to permit Brits and French and Spanish and Cypriots and Finns to carry on their businesses and get on with their lives in each other's countries in a way unthinkable in the previous two or three millennia of the chronicled existence of what we call Europe.

13

EUROPA, *MON AMOUR*

Our part of the world is named after Europa, a young Phoenician princess living in what today we would call Syria or Lebanon. She was abducted by the Greek god Zeus, who then ravished her.

After the 2005 Treaty was voted down, a new one was drafted with some minor changes and called the Treaty of Lisbon. The 1957 words 'ever-closer union' crept back in. To be honest, even as an EU nerd I paid no attention to the phrase 'ever-closer union of peoples'. I am sure none of my Conservative Eurosceptic friends came up to thank me for removing it before 2005 just as I am certain no Conservative made a fuss when the phrase popped back into the text in 2007.

Now like Lady Macbeth's damned spot, Mr Cameron wants the phrase out. This cannot be done without changing the Treaty, which requires a mammoth undertaking. The moment you sit down to rewrite a rule book every member of the club comes along with new suggestions and refuses to agree to what you or I might want unless we concede new rules desired by partners.

One-way traffic in rewriting rules – that is, one person dictates the new rules that suit his or her own beliefs or needs, and everyone else just shuts up and neither objects nor demands changes in rules that we don't want but someone else does – is fantasy negotiation.

It is a fantasy the rest of Europe is prepared to encourage Mr Cameron to indulge in, hoping that he will use his undoubted

PR skills to persuade his party, and then enough voters in our Eurosceptic nation, that we will be better off and stronger by voting to stay in the EU.

That is why the present government has been offered a pledge that when the time comes, as it will, for a new Treaty to be written, another appendix (called additional protocols in EU jargon) can be added to the 60-odd at the end of the Treaty, proclaiming that the 'ever-closer union of peoples' does not apply to us Brits.

It is both silly and a shame, but of such minor significance it can be given to Mr Cameron to keep him happy. In any event, he will no longer be prime minister when and if it happens.

PART THREE

14

THE EU'S SPRINGTIME FOR NATIONS

Yet another reason why I love the EU is that far from being the nation crusher of Tory/UKIP myth, or advancing inexorably towards becoming a federal super-state as Eurosceptics like William Hague told us was the end result of Tony Blair's cautious pro-European politics, the EU in my lifetime has been midwife to a latter-day springtime of nations in Europe in which we should all rejoice.

De Gaulle famously complained that it was impossible to govern a country – France – that produces 250 different cheeses. Today we have more independent nations and states than Europe has ever before. Baltic and Balkan states have emerged, as have Slovenia, Slovakia and the Czech Republic. Other nations like Scotland and Catalonia that are part of a bigger state have found a new identity, which has allowed them to assert their national traditions and cultures.

There are complaints that too many languages are spoken or used in the EU, and it's true that translation and interpretation are an additional cost. But how wonderful that the great languages of Europe, all of them with as much status and value as English or French or German, have a right to be used in the democratic debates and decisions of twenty-first-century Europe.

The growth of publishing, film-making, poetry, video, pop-up art exhibitions, murals, news media, books and creative arts in all the new nations and regions of Europe is something to be cherished and encouraged. A monolingual Britain will not do well in a multilingual world. Luckily we have not yet closed our borders, despite the xenophobic appeals of UKIP. Britain too has its medley of tongues, with Polish now the second language and Brit-Poles emerging as writers, film-makers and artists.

To be sure, I loved the bits of Europe I visited before my country joined Europe in 1973. I spent a lot of time in Portugal during the so-called 'carnations revolution' in 1974 when I marched with conscript soldiers in giant demonstrations in Lisbon, each young soldier with a flower sticking out of the barrel of his gun as they demonstrated for democracy and freedom and an end to the Portuguese empire.

Portugal joining the EU helped bed in that democracy. There are still problems galore in Portugal, as there are in every nation of Europe. Think of the young Ukrainians waving the yellow and blue flag of Europe as they occupied the centre of Kyiv and told Putin that the era of his oligarch cronies ruling Ukraine as a subordinate adjunct to Russia was over. Ukraine is too big and Europe is too tired right now, but somehow we must rediscover the spirit to let those who want democracy feel they have a home with the rest of us in the European Union.

Sunder Katwala, who runs British Future, one of the more original think-tanks in London working on issues of immigration and identity, argues in his lively pamphlet *How (Not) to Talk about Europe* (www.britishfuture.org) that one way to deal with fears about the arrival of many new EU citizens in poorer regions is to increase government funding for housing and training locally. He is right, but the same argument applies to new EU member states or would-be EU member states. They need help, not just in terms of solidarity, but so that they grow their economy as fast as possible and provide hope and work for their own citizens who then won't be impelled to leave home to work elsewhere in Europe.

To my regret, I have never had enough money to own a second home somewhere in Europe. But one of the great joys has been to see so many Brits buy a flat or chalet directly or via time-shares in different European countries. In Spain, Greece, France, Portugal, the Alps, the Canaries, the cheerful voice of England can be heard in every supermarket and in transplanted 'pubs', and the Europhobe *Daily Mail* is to be found on sale everywhere to keep the exiled Brits in touch with home passions.

So in every corner of Europe's foreign fields there is a place the Englishman and -woman calls home. To be sure, many Brits lived abroad before the EU was created; many have holiday homes in Florida or the Caribbean to repair to when the winter rains flood northern England and it's wiser to be lolling in the sun.

But the arrival in Europe of Brits from ordinary backgrounds who bought their council home in the 1980s or 1990s, sold or rented it and used the proceeds to move to southern Europe has transformed many lives. It is reckoned that up to 2 million UK passport holders live or work in the EU.

They can do so because European citizenship confers the unqualified right to enjoy the fruits of national citizenship. It is so taken for granted that no one stops to pause to examine how this small miracle has come about. No more negotiating for residence or work permits. No busy-body bureaucrat or municipal jobsworth to stop you owning a home, cultivating a garden, joining the local tennis club, getting a perma-tan on an Andalusian golf course, stoutly refusing to learn a word of Spanish or French and just getting on with your life as you did when living in Birmingham or Bootle.

This is a small, unsung miracle of EU existence, which I think is terrific and would hate to lose if the Brexit gang get their way. The EU's Maastricht Treaty (1992) makes clear that European citizenship is an add-on that all nationals of a EU member state enjoy. If we quit the EU we will lose this valuable right. I shall have to see if having family links to Ireland may entitle me to an Irish passport so that I remain an EU citizens as well as a British passport holder. But I would prefer it if I and my children and fellow citizens kept our European citizenship and the rights that come with it, by saying 'No' to Nigel Farage and the editor of the *Daily Mail*.

15

LIKE WORKERS, LOVE EUROPE

I am a lifelong trade unionist and joined my first trade union before I joined a political party. To admit to being pro-trade union is as toxic in some London circles as to admit to being pro-European. Trade unions have not always been in the right, but taken as a whole they delivered massive improvement for millions of people in the twentieth century.

Sometimes they were too political and often quite stupid. But in the constant search for harmony and social justice in the market economy, they were an essential part of delivering fairness. It is no accident that the astonishing rise in inequality in the twenty-first century, which at last is being taking seriously by influential commentators like Martin Wolf in the *Financial Times*, coincides with the weakening to the point of virtual elimination of trade unions in much of the capitalist world. In China and Russia, the petrol oligarch states and other authoritarian economies, trade unions in the sense of autonomous, independent, self-governing bodies of workers do not exist.

So I like the fact that the EU is the only grouping of nations in the world where supranational law protects workers' rights, imposes paid holidays and maternity leave and forbids any discrimination against disabled workers. Big companies that operate across two or more EU member states have to set up European Works Councils, so that worker representatives from all the countries can meet with the employers and discuss workplace problems.

Now let me be clear. This so-called Social Europe is no nirvana for workers, nor can Social Europe save trade unions if they no longer know how to recruit workers, or are über-politicized, or call strikes that hurt the public, not the owners of capital. The impact of technology, robots, mobile-phone booking and online shopping, combined with the failure to invest in training and education, especially in the UK, is hurting workers and lowering their incomes.

The answer is not to create new barriers to new products, or to try erect walls to stop workers crossing frontiers, but to reinvent worker rights and worker representation. The EU is a common market but also a set of rights that workers deserve. The TUC and British trade unions stopped Prime Minister Cameron from seeking to remove or reduce the UK's Social Europe obligations in his talks with Europe, even if the former prime minister, Sir John Major, and other right-wingers insisted that a reduction of Social Europe should be an object of Mr Cameron's new deal with Europe. If he wants to keep Britain in Europe, the Prime Minister needs every vote he can get to defeat the Tory/UKIP/Murdoch axis of relentless Europhobia. Mr Cameron is a pure-bred Tory so dislikes trade unions and Labour. But to win his plebiscite he need the support of the 6,400,000 British citizens who are trade union members and the 9,430,000 voters who supported Labour in May 2015.

16

A EUROPE FREE OF JUDICIAL MURDER

When I started my life as a political activist one of the big issues was the demand by right-wingers for the restoration of hanging. Ripe, port-sodden old Tories trembled at the knees in the excitement of their love affair with the rope. In pubs in working-class areas of Birmingham where I lived people would come with petitions to sign demanding a referendum on the restoration of capital punishment. I was certain then that had such a referendum been called the British public would have voted to bring back hanging. It is one of the many reason I don't like populist plebiscites.

One of the things I love best about Europe is that it enshrines as one of its core principles that no member state can execute its people. Unlike the death-row atrocities of the United States, where condemned men struggle in agony when lethal injections do not work properly, the EU has set its face against the judicial murder of its wrongdoers. That for me makes Europe a more civilized corner of the world to live in and I welcome that.

There is a famous remark attributed to the father of Indian independence, Mahatma Gandhi. In reply to the question 'What do you think of British civilization?', he said, 'I think it would be a good idea.' When I think of the European Union I think of civilization in the sense of the idea of so many people from so many nations using so many languages all able to live, trade, work, study, love, argue, write, paint, laugh and try and make the world a better place.

The EU has no magic bullet against mass population movements arising from the failure of national wars and invasions or the endemic poverty of corrupt nations whose citizens look to Europe for a job, safety and hope. It takes time to move from one dominant economic ideology to a different one more appropriate to new developments in technology, products and services.

Contrary to the myth, the EU does not run the individual economic policies of countries. Governments can spend as much as they like provided they raise the taxes to pay for their expenditure.

I would like to see a different, more growth- and job-focused EU. But the ruling elites in Europe are conservative men and women often wedded to yesterday's ideas. The way to change that is to engage politically and win support for better policies, not to walk out of Europe or denounce the EU as the cause of all ills in the style of a Marine Le Pen or Yanis Varoufakis.

Each European decision has to be signed off by 28 national governments with widely differing priorities, needs and views on how the world and their own nations should be run. As noted, the total income of the EU is just 1 per cent of Europe's GDP and 85 per cent of that goes back to nation states as agricultural subsidies and for developing poorer regions. So the money the EU has to spend itself is one sixth of 1 per cent of the Union's wealth. It's a lot of money, but far smaller than the Pentagon's budget and we get a lot more peace and social justice for our money than the Pentagon manages to create for America and the rest of the world.

So let us not turn away from Europe and let us not isolate our great country from our neighbours and friends. I feel much more strongly about Europe than these basic reasons can hope to express, but writing and reading about Europe can take to much time and life is too short.

I hope that if you have got this far you may have found reason enough to vote to remain linked to other European nations in the EU.

I would like the country I love to be confident and positive about the Europe I love and start being a player, partner and even a leading nation in the EU.

Above all I want those who come after me to have the privileges and good life as a European citizen that I have been able to enjoy in addition to the privilege of being born British.

CONCLUSION

HOPE AND SOLIDARITY: TWO GOOD EUROPEAN WORDS

I love the idea of Europe because I want to live in hope, not fear. Reactionary rightist politics are always pessimistic. Whatever world we inherit there is no need to change it, argue the reactionaries. As the Tory poet Alexander Pope put it: 'For forms of Government let fools contest; / Whate'er is best administer'd is best.' On the contrary, why and how we govern ourselves is at the heart of all human progress.

Reactionary leftist politics are equally pessimistic. For the unflinching left the foibles and failings of men and women have to be corrected by wiser leaders, philosopher-kings who form an all-knowing elite that seeks to iron out the warp and weft of the masses.

The Czechs have a saying that a pessimist is simply an optimist with up-to-date information but this *Mitteleuropa* cynicism is always trumped by Gramsci's pessimism of intelligence giving way to optimism of the will. Throughout postwar Britain, as the male elites contemplated the issue of integrating Europe to make war impossible and to allow peace, prosperity and progress to sink deeper and deeper roots in the country, there has been a steady pessimism of the intelligence, from the first days of the proposal to share sovereignty over coal and steel in 1950.

Labour Britain kept away from this project. In the splendid words of the great post-1945 Labour foreign secretary, Ernie Bevin, as he rejected the idea of any possible joint control over the then central coal and steel industries that produced energy and rebuilt Europe: 'If we open that Pandora's box, you never know what Trojan horses will jump out', he stated in a remarkable mixture of metaphors.

That dismissive pessimism has been a common thread linking different forms of Euroscepticism over the decades. Bevin was wrong in 1950 and those who project their pessimism on to twenty-first-century European construction are wrong now.

European union is not about faith. The moment humans invented forms of government they moved from faith to reality. It cannot be about charity, as charitable giving, while always worthwhile, cannot be a substitute for social justice and striving for equality. Europessimists dislike the idea of transfers between one state and another, even though the whole history of democratic government is a narrative of richer regions and richer individuals within a nation state helping out poorer regions and poorer people via various transfer payment systems, usually in the form of taxation.

Only four cantons in Switzerland – Zurich, Zug, Basel and Geneva – make money in the sense that the wealth they generate and taxes they raise are greater than their expenditure. All the other 20 cantons, including the federal capital of Berne, depend on transfers from the four rich cantons. The Swiss in their genius worked out centuries ago that they could only hold together if the rich supported the less well-off. If everyone wanted their money back the Helvetic confederation would collapse.

The same is true of poorer states within the United States, like Mississippi, which could not survive alone as economic entities and need the solidarity transfers of richer regions of America. So it is within states and so it is in a very modest, restrained way within Europe.

As an optimist I welcome the fact that since 1973 a minute helping of our national income has gone from Britain, a rich, net contributor to the EEC, now EU, to help grow Ireland, then Spain and Portugal and then 30 years later Poland.

That makes sense to me as a richer Ireland with good roads, housing, education, agriculture and various social and cultural projects paid from European funds has transformed Ireland from the breakaway, chippy, provincial nation freed from British rule but still so poor its sons and daughters had to cross the Irish Sea or the Atlantic to find work and hope into modern European Ireland, one of the best smaller nation states that you can find anywhere in the world.

In 1939, British money poured out of taxpayers' pockets to help Poland. It was called World War II. Today we pay a little to Poland (which in turn also contributes to the famous British rebate), and bit by bit Poland has more markets, more firms, more decent roads, more investment and soon we shall start missing the Poles who have come to the UK as the Irish did in the 1950s and 1960s. After 1945, 250,000 Poles stayed here, as Polish soldiers did not want to return to be enslaved by communism. In the 1990s after Solidarity helped bury communism and Poland became free, hundreds of thousands of Poles travelled here to work in the black labour market. After 2004 they became legal, paid taxes and National Insurance and today make an important net contribution to Her Majesty's Revenue and Customs.

The pessimists about Europe from Ernest Bevin to Enoch Powell would resent that financial transfer, or feel at best it should be an act of charity by rich England for its lost cousins in Ireland or its distant friends in Poland. Rather than charity, it is an act of solidarity seeking to make more equal the living standards between the countries. These financial transfers via the EU are a signal of hope that Britain and Ireland could shape a twenty-first century different from the previous ones of domination and resentment.

Ireland has not yet become rich enough to qualify as a net contributor to the EU budget, but one day it will reach that happy status and when it does, let us hope Irish optimism triumphs over pessimism, and that Ireland and the Irish understand that building a richer Europe, even if it means paying out a bit more than they get, is good for Ireland, just as Britain's net contribution to the common EU budget has been good for Britain.

Solidarity and hope. Two values that represent what living a decent life should be about. Getting proud nations and distinct peoples to show solidarity, one for the other, and to live in hope that cooperation not conflict will prevail is what constituted the founding principles of European integration after 1950. They remain as valid today as 66 years ago. On 23 June let us not turn our back on hope and on solidarity.

50 REASONS TO LOVE THE EU

Published by the *Independent* on the fiftieth anniversary of the Treaty of Rome.

1 The end of war between European nations
2 Democracy flourishing (more or less) in 28 countries
3 Once-poor countries have had a long period of prosperity
4 The creation of the world's largest internal trading market
5 Unparalleled rights for European consumers
6 Cooperation on a continent-wide immigration policy
7 Cooperation on crime, through Europol
8 Laws that make it easier for British people to buy property in Europe
9 Cleaner beaches and rivers throughout Europe
10 Four weeks statutory paid holiday a year for workers in Europe
11 No death penalty (it is incompatible with EU membership)
12 Competition from privatized companies means cheaper phone calls
13 Small EU bureaucracy (24,000 employees, fewer than the BBC)
14 Making the French eat British beef again
15 Minority languages, such as Irish, Welsh and Catalan recognized and protected
16 Europe is helping to save the planet with regulatory cuts in CO_2
17 One currency from Bantry to Berlin (but not Britain)

18 Europe-wide travel bans on tyrants such as Zimbabwe's Robert Mugabe

19 The EU gives twice as much aid to developing countries as the United States

20 Strict safety standards for cars, buses and aircraft

21 Free medical help for tourists

22 EU peacekeepers operate in trouble spots throughout the world

23 Europe's single market has brought cheap flights to the masses, and new prosperity for forgotten cities

24 Introduction of pet passports

25 It now takes only 2 hrs 35 mins from London to Paris by Eurostar

26 Prospect of EU membership has forced modernization on Turkey

27 Shopping without frontiers gives consumers more power to shape markets

28 Cheap travel and study programmes mean greater mobility for Europe's youth

29 Food labelling is much clearer

30 No tiresome border checks (apart from in the UK)

31 Compensation for passengers suffering air delays

32 Strict ban on animal testing for the cosmetics industry

33 Greater protection for Europe's wildlife

34 Regional development fund has aided the deprived parts of Britain

35 European driving licences recognized across the EU

36 Britons now feel a lot less insular

37 Europe's bananas remain bent, despite sceptics' fears

38 Strong economic growth – greater than the USA last year

39 Single market has brought the best continental footballers to Britain

40 Human rights legislation has protected the rights of the individual

41 European Parliament provides democratic checks on all EU laws

42 EU gives more, not less, sovereignty to nation states

43 Maturing EU is a proper counterweight to the power of the USA and China

44 European immigration has boosted the British economy

45 Europeans are increasingly multilingual – except Britons, who are less so
46 Europe has set Britain an example of how properly to fund a national health service
47 British restaurants now much more cosmopolitan
48 Total mobility for career professionals in Europe
49 Europe has revolutionized British attitudes to food and cooking
50 Lists like this drive the Eurosceptics mad